Jam Session

Derek Jeter

Terri Dougherty
ABDO Publishing Company

visit us at
www.abdopub.com

Published by ABDO Publishing Company, 4940 Viking Drive, Suite 622, Edina, Minnesota 55435. Copyright © 2000 by Abdo Consulting Group, Inc. International copyrights reserved in all countries. No part of this book may be reproduced in any form without written permission from the publisher.

Printed in the United States.

Cover and Interior Photo credits: AP Wide World Photos; All-Sport Photos

Edited by Denis Dougherty

Sources: Associated Press; New York Times; New York Daily News; Sports Illustrated; Sports Illustrated For Kids; Time Magazine; ESPN Magazine

Library of Congress Cataloging-in-Publication Data

Dougherty, Terri.
    Derek Jeter / Terri Dougherty.
        p.   cm. -- (Jam Session)
    Includes index.
    Summary: Discusses the personal life and baseball career of the young man from Michigan who plays shortstop for the New York Yankees.
      ISBN 1-57765-366-1 (hardcover)
      ISBN 1-57765-367-X (paperback)
    1. Jeter, Derek, 1974-   --Juvenile literature.   2. Baseball players--United States--Biography--Juvenile literature. [1. Jeter, Derek, 1974- . 2. Baseball players. 3. Racially mixed people--Biography] I. Title. II. Series.
    GV865.J48 D68   2000
    796.323'092--dc21
    [B]   99-046526
                                                                      CIP
                                                                       AC

Contents

Hero and Heartthrob

Derek Jeter is living his dream. As a little boy, he adored the New York Yankees. He loved seeing them play at Yankee Stadium. He watched them on television. Derek idolized legendary Yankee outfielder Dave Winfield and had a poster of Winfield on his bedroom wall.

Now, Derek is wearing Yankee pinstripes and starring at shortstop for the team he cheered for as a child. "I was always telling people that I was going to play for the Yankees someday," Derek said. "I think I'm the luckiest person in the world.

"I have the greatest job in the world," he said. "Only one person can have it. You have shortstops on other teams—I'm not knocking other teams—but there's only one shortstop on the Yankees."

Derek is more than just a baseball player in New York. He's a celebrity who is almost as well-known for his good looks as for his ability to play baseball. He dated pop singer Mariah Carey, and when he takes the field he's greeted by screams and marriage proposals from girls who love his pale green eyes.

People admire the talented shortstop because of his work ethic and composure. He's able to keep a level head in the middle of all the attention. "Jeter is a very special guy," Yankees manager Joe Torre said. "There's something about his presence that makes you feel good."

When Derek walks out to the field he sees a sign with a quote from Yankees legend Joe DiMaggio, "I want to thank the good Lord for making me a Yankee." Derek couldn't agree more.

Detroit Tigers' Jason Wood is forced out at second base by Derek Jeter.

A Shy Guy

Derek was born in Pequannock, New Jersey, and grew up with his parents and younger sister, Sharlee, in Kalamazoo, Michigan. He loved playing basketball and baseball, but was shy around other kids.

"When he was 12 or 13, I took him to a basketball camp at the University of Michigan," recalled his dad, Charles Jeter. "When it was time for him to meet the other kids, I had to push him to make conversation.

"When he was in the eighth grade and was about to switch from parochial school to a public school, we sent him over to the YMCA to play basketball against older kids as a way of toughening him up," Charles said. "He went, but he took his mother with him."

Derek's dad is a drug and alcohol counselor, and his mom, Dorothy, is an accountant. His dad is African American, and his mom is Irish American. Because Derek and his sister had a black father and a white mother, the Jeter kids weren't always treated kindly.

Derek was already in a baseball uniform at age five.

"As a biracial family, you get a lot of those stares," Charles said. "You can't live in this world without running into ignorant people, and we felt our children were sometimes left out of social situations—all-star teams, things like that—for racial reasons. We would just tell Sharlee and Derek, 'You've got to be good, and for some people you've got to be better.'"

Derek posing with his family.

Derek sees his heritage as an advantage. "No one knows what I am, so I can relate to everyone," Derek said. "I've got all kinds of friends: black, white, and Spanish."

Derek's family is very close. Even though his parents were very strict, he respected their rules. "He had a lot of friends who could do whatever they wanted—stay out late, even the night before a game—but our curfews were always the earliest," Sharlee said.

Charles and Dorothy taught their children to be humble and stressed hard work and determination. "My parents taught me that the harder you work, the better you'll be," Derek said.

In the summer, Derek visited his grandmother and other relatives in New Jersey. His grandmother was a Yankee fan, and she turned Derek into one, too. His dad played shortstop at Fisk University, so that was the position Derek played in Little League. "I always wanted to be like my dad," Derek said.

Pros and Cons

Derek, known as D.J. in Kalamazoo, graduated from Kalamazoo Central High School in 1992. He hit .557 with seven home runs as a junior and .508 with four home runs as a senior. He was 12-for-12 in stolen bases and was named the 1992 High School Player of the Year by the American Baseball Coaches Association.

Scouts from 27 major-league teams watched Derek play his senior year. Yankees scout Dick Groch was amazed at Jeter's talent as a high school sophomore. "I see an electric body," Groch said. "Thin, but with lithe, sinewy muscle. Classic infielder's body type. Fluid and graceful."

Groch thought Derek had the ability to be the greatest shortstop in Yankees history and the leader of a championship team. "A player like this makes you hyperventilate," he said.

Nine-year-old Derek, wearing his Little League uniform, gets ready to bat.

The Yankees believed Groch and chose Derek with their first-round pick in the June 1992 free-agent draft. Derek was the sixth pick overall, and the first high school player chosen.

"When he was in Little League, he said he was going to play for the Yankees," Charles Jeter said. "It's amazing the Yankees drafted him in the first round."

Derek was a Yankee, but he wasn't ready for the big leagues yet. He started the 1992 season in Tampa, Florida, and played 47 games in the Rookie League. He hit just .202 with three home runs, but was moved up to Class A in Greensboro, North Carolina, for the last two weeks of the season.

Derek was getting his first taste of the baseball career he had hoped for, but he was miserable. "I cried in my room every night," Derek said. "I'd never been away from home before, and I didn't feel like I belonged. I felt overmatched."

His teammates had a different opinion, however. "He could play," said catcher Jorge Posada, a teammate of Derek's at Greensboro in 1992 and later with the Yankees. "There was no doubt."

A Major Change

*T*he Yankees invited Derek to big league spring training the next season. He was in awe as he played alongside Don Mattingly, Wade Boggs, and Paul O'Neill.

"I'm 19, and throwing to Don Mattingly," Derek said. "I'm going from Kalamazoo Central High School—with a friend at third and another friend at first—and here I am at spring training, with Wade Boggs to my right, and I'm throwing to Don Mattingly. I couldn't believe it!"

Working out with the Yankees stars gave Derek confidence. "I saw I had the ability to make it," Derek said. "I also saw how hard I would have to work."

Mattingly taught Derek something about hard work when they were returning to the clubhouse after

Derek won the 1994 Minor League Player of the Year award.

running sprints. "We had to cross the main field to get to the clubhouse," Derek said. "There's nobody there—no fans, not even the grounds crew. So we were walking. And Mattingly tells me we'd better run, because you never know who's watching. This is Don Mattingly! Who's going to tell him he has to run? That made a big impression on me. Since that day, when I'm on the field, I always run."

Derek spent the 1993 season at Greensboro, hitting .295 with five home runs, and moved around the next season. He started in Tampa, hitting .329. Then, he played at Albany, New York, where he batted .377, and Columbus, Ohio, where he hit .349.

He batted .317 at Columbus in 1995, and got his shot at the major leagues. He was called up by the Yankees for 15 games and batted .250. He sat next to his friend Posada in the dugout as the Yankees went after the American League wild-card playoff berth.

"We were like little kids," Posada said. "We kept telling each other, 'Man, this is the big leagues, this is unbelievable. We have to get here and, next time, we have to stay.'"

Pride and Poise in Pinstripes

Derek burst on the major-league scene as the Yankees starting shortstop the next season. He showed rare composure for a rookie playing the most important position on a team that is always in the spotlight.

Joe Torre didn't expect anything special from Derek that year. He said he'd be happy if Derek played good defense and hit .250. But that wasn't what Derek expected of himself.

"I didn't expect to do anything different than I did in the minors," said Derek, who hit .306 in four minor-league seasons.

Torre was surprised by the confident way Derek charged the ball. "That was unusual for a kid that young," Torre said. "As I soon learned, though, he had a maturity unlike any other 21-year-old I'd ever seen. There was a presence about him that led me to believe he was going to develop quickly as a big-leaguer."

Derek takes time to sign autographs before a game.

Derek was the Yankees' first rookie shortstop to start on opening day since 1962, but he didn't seem nervous. His poise was evident when Cleveland's Omar Vizquel hit a blooper toward the outfield. It seemed too deep for Derek, but he turned, sprinted, and followed the ball perfectly. At just the right moment, he made an acrobatic move, reached over his left shoulder and caught the ball. His catch saved a run.

"I kept running and running, and then I got to it. I just made up my mind I wanted the ball hit to me," Derek said.

"That was a major-league play," Yankees pitcher David Cone said. "Right then and there we all learned something about Derek."

Derek celebrates after hitting a home run.

Derek's talent, work habits, and instinct for the game made him play like a veteran. "He's unusual," said Willie Randolph, the Yankees third-base coach and a former all-star infielder. "You can tell by the way a guy carries himself—like he belongs. He's not afraid to make the big play. He doesn't scare."

But Derek didn't do everything right that season. In the top of the 10th inning in a game against the Chicago White Sox, he caught a ground ball and threw it over the first baseman's head. It bounced into the stands. The Yankees lost 8-4. "That inexperience is going to show up once in a while," Torre said. "But he's played his tail off and won so many games for us, the scale is weighing heavily in our favor."

Derek batted .314 that season. He hit an inside-the-park home run on August 2, against Kansas City. It was one of 10 home runs he hit that season. He had a 17-game hitting streak, the longest by a Yankees rookie since DiMaggio's 18-game streak in 1936. Derek had 78 RBI and led the club with 183 hits, two triples, and 156 games started. He was named AL Rookie of the Year by the Baseball Writers Association.

But Derek didn't let success go to his head because, "If I want to go home, I can't do that. In our house, we learned not to talk about yourself. I don't like people who talk about themselves."

Derek waits for the pitch.

On Top of the World

As exciting as Derek's rookie season was, he saved the best for last. The Yankees pounded their way through the playoffs and won their first World Series title since 1978. On the way to the World Series, Derek took part in one of the most controversial plays in major-league history.

It happened in the first game of the American League Championship Series, when Derek hit a home run in Yankee Stadium. His long fly ball soared toward a young fan who reached over the fence and grabbed the ball. Perhaps the Baltimore right fielder could have caught it if the fan hadn't reached out, but the umpire signaled home run. Derek's homer tied the score 4-4, and the Yankees went on to win 5-4.

The Yankees faced the defending champion Atlanta Braves in the World Series. Even though Derek was a rookie, his manager knew he could handle the pressure. "He doesn't see the postseason as something different. Derek knows how to be serious and he knows how to have fun," Torre said. "That's important."

After losing the first two games in New York, the Yankees rebounded to win the next three in Atlanta. They clinched the title in Game 6 in New York. "It was like a dream when we won," said Derek, who batted .361 and scored 12 runs in the postseason.

"I was always a Yankee fan growing up, and it was my dream to play for them, and then we won everything my first year," he said. "A lot of people play their whole career and never get that chance. I was very fortunate."

Derek reacts after striking out.

Shortstop Stands Tall among Yankees

By his second season in the majors, Derek was well on his way to making his mark with the Yankees. "Jeter is the next leader of this ball club," Torre said.

In his first and second seasons, he scored more than 100 runs. DiMaggio was the only other Yankee to accomplish that feat.

"It's overwhelming at times," Derek said. "It's like everything happened so fast. My first year, everything happened. We won the World Series, the Rookie of the Year, everything came so quick. It's like everything's been in fast-forward."

In a 1997 division series, Derek had two homers and hit .333. But the Yankees were eliminated by the Cleveland Indians.

Derek continued to enjoy playing and working hard. "A ballplayer plays every day, and it's a very humbling sport," Derek said. "One day you can do great and the next day you can do terrible, or you can do everything right and still not be successful."

Derek kept his goals to himself. "I've always been like that. It seems people have been doubting me as long as I've been playing. Like, I come from Kalamazoo and people say, 'How can he possibly play professional baseball?' So, I like the challenge."

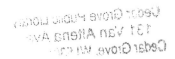

Derek fires the ball to first base.

Year of the Yankees

Derek's power and poise continued to dazzle his teammates and fans the next season. His .324 batting average was fifth in the AL. He hit 19 home runs, breaking Roy Smalley's single-season home run record for Yankees shortstops. He finished third in voting for AL Most Valuable Player and was named to his first All-Star team.

"He's an outstanding young talent," David Cone said. "I'm not sure what more you want from a shortstop. He makes all the plays—he really leaves a pitcher feeling good out there—gets his hits, gets his RBIs. He's a complete package."

"Derek's power can be unbelievable," added Yankees first baseman Tino Martinez. Derek was a key part of the winningest team of all time in 1998. The Yankees won 114 games in the regular season and a total of 125, including the postseason.

"He's a very confident young man, and he has the wherewithal to back it up," Torre said. "He's not caught up in his celebrity or stardom. He knows what comes first."

"Derek has a tremendous amount of talent. The sky's the limit for him," Yankees second baseman Chuck Knoblauch said. "He's easy to get along with, and he has that smile."

The Yankees beat the Texas Rangers in a division series and faced the Cleveland Indians in the ALCS. Derek had a two-run triple in the sixth inning of Game 6 as the Yankees won 9-5 to take the series. "The team had been ready for this moment all season," Derek said.

New York faced San Diego in the World Series. "The approach isn't different," Derek said. "This team doesn't like to lose. Everybody keeps the same approach and the same intensity level against everybody."

The Yankees won the first three games of the series and were looking for a sweep. In Game 4, the score was 0-0 when Derek hit a high bouncer toward the shortstop. He ran as fast as he could to first base and beat the throw.

Derek and his teammates meet President Clinton after the Yankees win the 1998 World Series.

Paul O'Neill hit a fastball into the right-field corner, and Derek raced to third. Bernie Williams hit a high chopper toward the pitcher's mound, and Derek was off toward home. He slid across the plate, knocking catcher Carlos Hernandez off his feet.

In the eighth inning, Derek led off with a walk. O'Neill's single sent him to second, and he reached third on a ground out by Williams. Derek scored on a sacrifice fly, and the Yankees went on to win 3-0. They were champions again!

Derek, who batted .353 in the series, waved two fingers at screaming Yankees fans. In the clubhouse, he hugged O'Neill. He had ended another fairy-tale season in storybook fashion.

Opposite page: Derek reacts to a seventh-inning grand slam from Tino Martinez during Game 1 of the 1998 World Series.

Big Man in the Big Apple

Derek's stock continued to soar in 1999, on and off the field. He led the major leagues in hits (219) and was second in the AL in batting (.349). He tied for second in the AL in runs (134) and triples (nine). The Yankees finished with the best record in the AL, and Derek led his team back to the postseason.

Derek was his usual self in the playoffs, hitting home runs and playing spectacular defense. The Yankees followed Derek's lead cruising to their third World Series in the past four years and their unbelievable record 25th World Series title in franchise history.

The Yankees couldn't be stopped. They swept the Texas Rangers in the Divisional playoffs. In the ALCS they hammered the Boston Red Sox four games to one. In what was supposed to be a competitive World Series against the Atlanta Braves, the Yankees took control and never let go, sweeping the National League Champions.

Derek has done it all on the baseball field. But he knows that there is more to life than just baseball. Derek is helping others through his success. His Turn 2 Foundation, which his father runs, works to steer high-risk kids away from drugs. The work of his childhood idol, Winfield, inspired him to start the foundation.

Derek is surprised by the attention he attracts. "It has been overwhelming," he said. "It's something I never expected, but I'm having a great time with it."

His teammates say he will be a great player for many years. "He's the future captain of the Yankees, if he's not already," Cone said. "And let's not forget, most of all, he leads us by what he does with his bat, his glove, and his legs. He just keeps getting better and better."

O'Neill added, "By the time Derek's finished, we are all going to say he's the best player we've ever played with."

Derek watches his home run against Cleveland.

Derek Jeter Profile

Born: June 26, 1974, in

Pequannock, New Jersey

Height: 6-foot-3

Weight: 195 pounds

Position: Shortstop

Bats: Right

Throws: Right

Resides: Tampa, Florida

Family: Father, Charles; Mother,

Dorothy; sister, Sharlee

Personal: Attends the University

of Michigan in the off-season ... is best

friends with Seattle Mariners all-star shortstop Alex Rodriguez ...

has the nickname D.J. ... enjoys going to movies ... favorite sport

to watch and play, other than baseball, is basketball ... favorite

food is chicken parmesan ... favorite color is blue ... math was an

easy subject for him in school ... likes visiting Puerto Rico ... has a

fear of animals ... named one of *People* magazine's 50 Most

Beautiful People in the World in 1997 and 1999.

Derek Jeter's Regular Season Stats

Year	Avg.	Runs	SB	HR	RBI
1995	.250	5	0	0	7
1996	.314	104	14	10	78
1997	.291	116	23	10	70
1998	.324	127	30	19	84
1999	.349	134	19	24	102

KEY: Avg. - Batting average; SB - Stolen bases; HR - Home runs; RBI - Runs batted in.

Jeter blasts a two-run homer.

Derek Jeter Chronology

June 26, 1974 - Derek Sanderson Jeter is born in Pequannock, New Jersey.

1992 - Graduates from Kalamazoo (Michigan) Central High School. Named High School Player of the Year by the American Baseball Coaches Association. Signed by New York Yankees after team selected him with sixth overall pick in June free-agent draft. Begins pro career in Tampa, Florida.

1993 - Voted Most Outstanding Major League Prospect by South Atlantic League managers.

1994 - Named Minor League Player of the Year by several publications.

1995 - Makes big-league debut, playing in 15 games.

1996 - Becomes Yankees' first rookie shortstop to start on opening day since 1962. Named AL Rookie of the Year. Helps Yankees to first World Series championship since 1978.

1997 - Scores 116 runs, becoming only Yankees player other than Joe DiMaggio to score more than 100 runs in his first two seasons. Wins Joan Payson Award for community service, an honor given each year by New York's baseball writers, for visiting kids in hospitals and his Turn 2 Foundation. Named one of the world's 50 most beautiful people by *People* magazine.

1998 - Finishes third in voting for the AL's MVP. Named to all-star team. Helps Yankees to World Series title and a record 125 victories, including postseason.

Derek Jeter completes a sixth-inning double play as the Cleveland Indians' Manny Ramirez slides into second base.

Glossary

AL - American League, one of the two organizations (along with the National League) that make up Major League Baseball, the highest level of professional baseball. The AL and NL are also called the "big leagues" or "major leagues."

ALCS - American League Championship Series. It is a best-of-seven playoff series to determine the AL champion, with the winner advancing to the World Series.

BATTING AVERAGE - A ratio (as a rate per thousand) of hits to official times at bat. When it is said a player "hit" or "batted" .324, for example, it is a reference to the player's batting average.

DIVISION SERIES - A first-round, best-of-five playoff series. The winner advances to the league championship series.

HIT - To reach base safely by hitting the ball.

HOME RUN - A hit that allows the batter to reach home plate safely. Almost always, the ball is hit out of the field of play. Also called a homer.

INSIDE-THE-PARK HOME RUN - A home run that occurs when a batter does not hit the ball out of the field of play, but is still able to reach home plate safely.

MINOR LEAGUE - A group of professional teams in a league below the major leagues.

MVP - Most Valuable Player.

RBI - Runs batted in. It occurs when a batter's performance enables a teammate to score a run.

RUN - A score in baseball. It occurs when a player reaches home plate safely.

SHORTSTOP - Plays between second and third base. Fields ground balls, line drives, and popups. Also throws out and tags runners and turns the double play.

STOLEN BASE - To run to the next base without the ball being hit.

TRIPLE - A hit that allows the batter to reach third base safely.

WORLD SERIES - A best-of-seven series to determine the champion of Major League Baseball. It matches the AL and NL champions.

Jeter dives for the ball.

Index